Talking Hands

DAYS AND TIMES

DÍAS Y HORAS

WRITTEN BY KATHLEEN PETELINSEK AND E. RUSSELL PRIMM
ILLUSTRATED BY NICHOLE DAY DIGGINS

A SPECIAL THANKS TO OUR ADVISERS: JUNE PRUSAK IS A DEAF THERAPEUTIC RECREATOR WHO
BELIEVES IN THE MOTTO "LIFE IS GOOD," REGARDLESS OF YOUR ABILITY TO HEAR.

CARMINE L. VOZZOLO IS AN EDUCATOR WHO WORKS WITH CHILDREN
WHO ARE DEAF OR HARD OF HEARING AND THEIR FAMILIES.

The Child's World

Published in the United States of America by The Child's World®
PO Box 326, Chanhassen, MN 55317-0326
800-599-READ
www.childsworld.com

Cover / frontispiece: left—Photodisc; right—Comstock Images.

Interior: 3, 4, 7, 8, 16, 18, 19—Photodisc; 5—Cooperphoto / Corbis; 6, 9, 15—Burke / Triolo Productions / Brand X Pictures; 10—Image Source / Punchstock; 11, 12, 13, 21—Stockdisc; 14—Kathleen Petelinsek; 17—Comstock Images; 20—RubberBall Productions; 22—C Squared Studios / Photodisc / Getty Images; 23—Purestock / Punchstock.

The Child's World®: Mary Berendes, Publishing Director

Editorial Directions, Inc.: E. Russell Primm, Editorial Director; Katie Marsico, Project Editor and Managing Editor; Caroline Wood, Editorial Assistant; Javier Millán, Proofreader; Cian Laughlin O'Day, Photo Researcher and Selector

The Design Lab: Kathleen Petelinsek, Art Director; Julia Goozen, Art Production

LIBRARY OF CONGRESS CATALOGING-IN-PUBLICATION DATA
Petelinsek, Kathleen.
  Days and times = Días y horas / by Kathleen Petelinsek and E. Russell Primm.
    p. cm. — (Talking hands)
  Summary: Provides illustrations of American Sign Language signs and Spanish and English text for words related to days and time.
  In English, Spanish, and American Sign Language.
  ISBN 1-59296-681-0 (lib. bdg. : alk. paper)
  1. American Sign Language—Vocabulary—Juvenile literature. 2. Spanish language—Vocabulary—Juvenile literature. 3. Days—Juvenile literature. 4. Time—Juvenile literature. I. Primm, E. Russell, 1958–. II. Title. III. Title: Días y horas. IV. Series: Petelinsek, Kathleen. Talking hands.
  HV2476.P4732 2006
  419'.7082461—dc22   2006009035

NOTE TO PARENTS AND EDUCATORS:

The understanding of any language begins with the acquisition of vocabulary, whether the language is spoken or manual. The books in the Talking Hands series provide readers, both young and old, with a first introduction to basic American Sign Language signs. Combining close photo cues and simple, but detailed, line illustration, children and adults alike can begin the process of learning American Sign Language. In addition to the English word and sign for that word, we have included the Spanish word. The addition of the Spanish word is a wonderful way to allow children to see multiple ways (English, Spanish, signed) to say the same word. This is also beneficial for Spanish-speaking families to learn the sign even though they may not know the English word for that object.

Let these books be an introduction to the world of American Sign Language. Most languages have regional dialects and multiple ways of expressing the same thought. This is also true for sign language. We have attempted to use the most common version of the signs for the words in this series. As with any language, the best way to learn is to be taught in person by a frequent user. It is our hope that this series will pique your interest in sign language.

Time
Hora

1.

2.

Tap wrist with index finger. Repeat.

Golpea la muñeca ligeramente
con el dedo índice. Repetir.

3

Second
Segundo

1.

2.

3.

Fingers spell S-E-C.
Los dedos deletrean S-E-C.

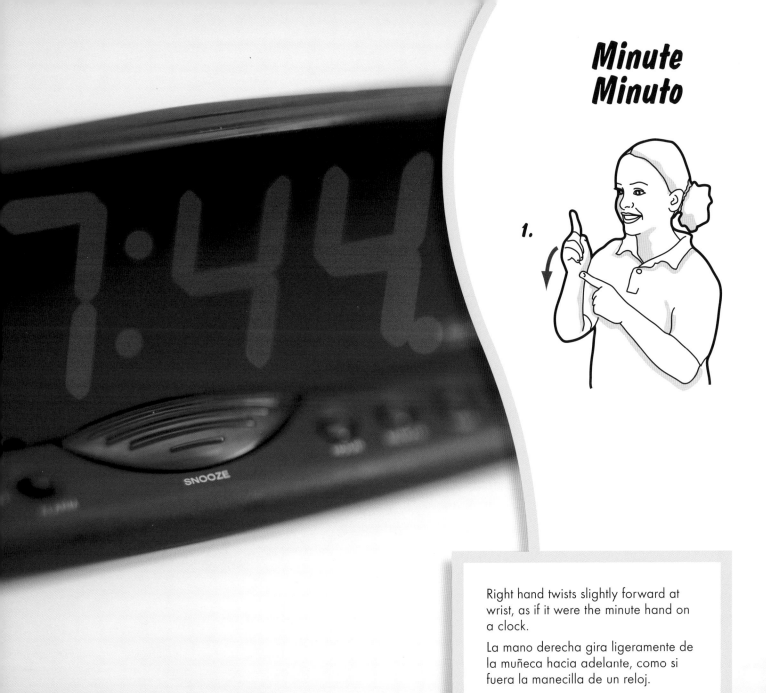

Minute
Minuto

1.

Right hand twists slightly forward at wrist, as if it were the minute hand on a clock.

La mano derecha gira ligeramente de la muñeca hacia adelante, como si fuera la manecilla de un reloj.

5

Hour
Hora

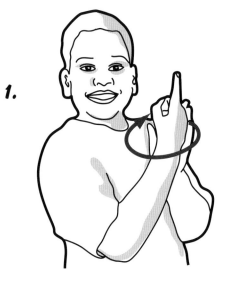

1.

Right hand makes the "1" hand shape, and pinky side of right hand touches palm of open left hand. Move right hand in a circular motion and end in the starting position.

La mano derecha forma el "1" y el lado rotado de la mano toca la palma abierta de la mano izquierda. Mover la mano derecha en forma circular y terminar en la posición al comenzar.

Morning
Mañana

1.

Flat left hand is placed on the inside of right elbow.
Flat right hand arcs up and toward body.

La mano izquierda plana se pone en la parte de
adentro del codo derecho. La mano derecha plana
se arquea hacia arriba y hacia el cuerpo.

Afternoon
Tarde

1.

Both hands are flat (with palms facing down). Right arm is angled out and away from body. Index finger of left hand touches right elbow.

Ambas manos planas (palmas hacia abajo). Brazo derecho en ángulo hacia afuera y alejado del cuerpo. Dedo índice izquierdo toca el codo derecho.

Night
Noche

1.

Both hands are flat. Right arm is bent at wrist.

Las dos manos planas. El brazo derecho está doblado de en la muñeca.

Day
Día

1.

2.

Right arm makes the "1" hand shape and goes from pointing straight up to touching left arm.

Formar el "1" con el brazo derecho, apuntar hacia arriba haste tocar el brazo izquierdo.

Early
Temprano

Fingers spell E-A-R-L-Y in a circular motion. Start from right shoulder and move clockwise.

Los dedos deletrean E-A-R-L-Y en forma circular. Empezar del hombro derecho y mover en el sentido de las agujas del reloj.

Late
Tarde

1.

Right hand is flat. Right arm is bent at elbow and swings toward back.

La mano derecha está plana. El brazo derecho está encurvado del codo y mover hacia atrás.

Later
Después/Más Tarde

1.

2.

Right hand makes the "L" hand shape. Thumb of right hand is on the palm of left hand. Right hand twists from pointing up to pointing down.

La mano derecha forma la "L." El pulgar de la mano derecha está en la palma de la mano izquierda. La mano derecha gira de arriba para abajo.

Week
Semana

1.

2.

Chores

SUN	MON	TUES	WED	THURS	FRI	SAT
Grocery Shopping with Mom	Mow the Lawn	Violin Practice	Wash Dishes	Take out the garbage	Basketball Practice	

Right hand makes the "1" hand shape. Right hand begins on left palm and slides off this hand.

La mano derecha forma el "1." La mano derecha empieza en la palma de la mano izquierda y se desliza hacia afuera de este mano.

Sunday
Domingo

1.

Open hands face forward. Move both hands in, up, and out in a circular path.

Las manos abiertas hacia adelante. Mover ambas manos hacia adentro, arriba, y afuera en trayectoria circular.

Monday
Lunes

1.

Right hand makes the "M" hand shape (with fingertips facing body) and moves in circles.

Formar la "M" con la mano (con las yemas de los dedos mirando hacia el cuerpo) y mover la mano en círculos.

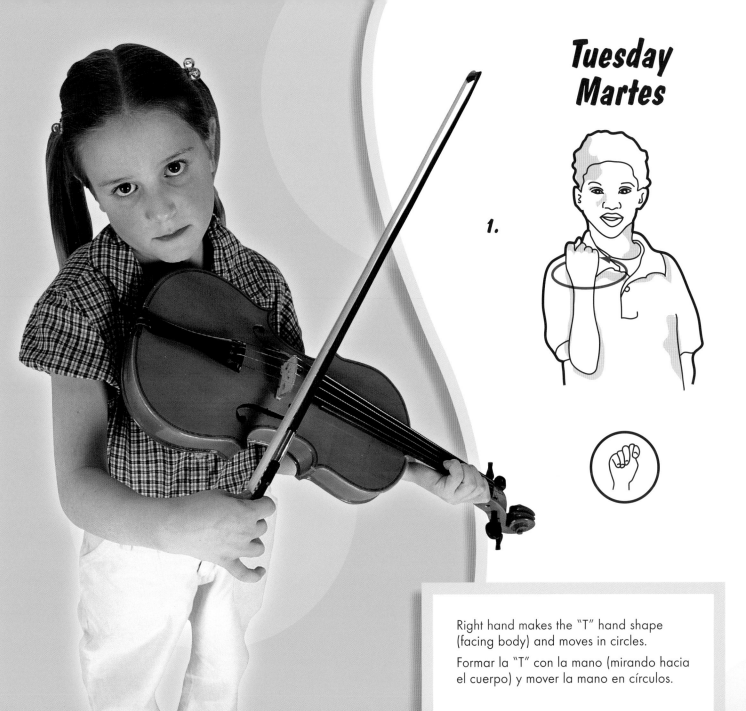

Tuesday
Martes

1.

Right hand makes the "T" hand shape (facing body) and moves in circles.

Formar la "T" con la mano (mirando hacia el cuerpo) y mover la mano en círculos.

17

Wednesday
Miércoles

1.

Right hand makes the "W" hand shape (with palm facing body) and moves in circles.

Formar la "W" con la mano (palma mirando hacia el cuerpo) y mover la mano en círculos.

Thursday
Jueves

1.

2.

Right hand makes the "T" hand shape. It then makes the "H" hand shape. Repeat.

Formar la "T" con la mano. Luego formar la "H" con la mano. Repetir.

19

Friday
Viernes

1.

Right hand makes the "F" hand shape (with palm facing body) and moves in circles.

Formar la "F" con la mano (palma mirando hacia el cuerpo) y mover en círculos.

Saturday
Sábado

1.

Right hand makes the "S" hand shape (with palm facing body) and moves in circles.

Formar la "S" con la mano (palma mirando hacia el cuerpo) y mover la mano en círculos.

21

Month
Mes

1.

2.

Both hands make the "1" hand shape. Left hand points up and stays still while right index finger points left and slides down once.

Ambas manos forman el "1." La mano izquierda señala hacia arriba y se mantiene inmóvil mientras el dedo índice derecho señala a la izquierda y se desliza hacia abajo una sola vez.

Year
Año

1.

Both hands make the "S" hand shape. Left hand stays still while right hand moves forward in a circle. End in the starting position.

Ambas manos forman la "S." La mano izquierda se mantiene inmóvil mientras que la mano derecha se mueve hacia adelante en un círculo. Terminar en la posición al comenzar.

A B C D E F

G H I J K

L M N O P

Q R S T U

V W X Y Z